ANIMALS IN THE CITY

Skunks

Ava Podmorow

Explore other books at:
WWW.ENGAGEBOOKS.COM

VANCOUVER, B.C.

WWW.ENGAGEBOOKS.COM

Skunks: Level Pre-1
Animals in the City
Podmorow, Ava 2004 –
Text © 2022 Engage Books
Design © 2022 Engage Books

Edited by: A.R. Roumanis
and Sarah Harvey

Text set in Epilogue

FIRST EDITION / FIRST PRINTING

LIBRARY AND ARCHIVES CANADA CATALOGUING IN PUBLICATION

Title: Skunks / Ava Podmorow.
Names: Podmorow, Ava, author.
Description: Series statement: Animals in the city
Engaging readers: level pre-1, beginner.

Identifiers: Canadiana (print) 20220398666 | Canadiana (ebook) 20220398674
ISBN 978-1-77476-748-1 (hardcover)
ISBN 978-1-77476-749-8 (softcover)
ISBN 978-1-77476-750-4 (epub)
ISBN 978-1-77476-751-1 (pdf)

Subjects:
LCSH: Readers (Elementary)
LCSH: Readers—Skunks.
LCGFT: Readers (Publications)

Classification: LCC PE1119.2 .P645 2022 | DDC J428.6/2—DC23

This project has been made possible in part
by the Government of Canada.

Canada

Watch out for that skunk!

3

Skunks love living in cities.

Some skunks even live under decks and in garages!

Skunks are excellent diggers.

They dig holes in the ground called dens.

Skunks sometimes dig their dens in lawns or in gardens.

Skunks have babies in dens in the spring.

They can have four to six babies at a time.

Baby skunks are called kits.

Kits stay with their mothers until they are about four months old.

Then they are able to
set off on their own.

Skunks like to eat fruits, vegetables or small animals like mice.

Skunks can be helpful to farmers.

They eat pests that
live in farmers' fields.

The striped skunk is the most common kind of skunk.

Skunks have long sharp claws for digging.

Claws

They have sprayers under their big fluffy tails.

Tail

Sprayer

23

Skunks spray when they feel they are in danger.

When a skunk lifts its tail, it is about to spray.

Back away from the spray!

Explore other books in the Animals In The City series.

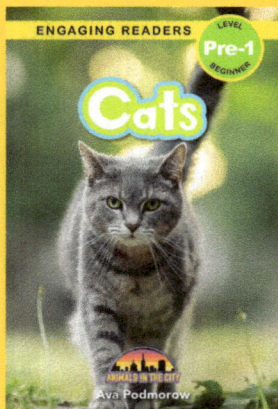

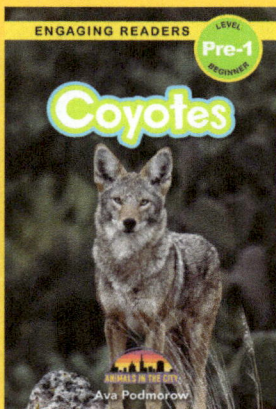

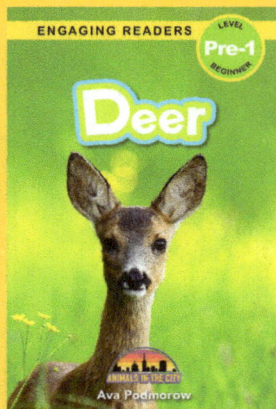

ENGAGING READERS
LEVEL Pre-1 BEGINNER
Cats
ANIMALS IN THE CITY
Ava Podmorow

ENGAGING READERS
LEVEL Pre-1 BEGINNER
Coyotes
ANIMALS IN THE CITY
Ava Podmorow

ENGAGING READERS
LEVEL Pre-1 BEGINNER
Deer
ANIMALS IN THE CITY
Ava Podmorow

ENGAGING READERS
LEVEL Pre-1 BEGINNER
Owls
ANIMALS IN THE CITY
Ava Podmorow

ENGAGING READERS
LEVEL Pre-1 BEGINNER
Pigeons
ANIMALS IN THE CITY
Ava Podmorow

ENGAGING READERS
LEVEL Pre-1 BEGINNER
Rabbits
ANIMALS IN THE CITY
Ava Podmorow

ENGAGING READERS
LEVEL Pre-1 BEGINNER
Raccoons
ANIMALS IN THE CITY
Sarah Harvey

ENGAGING READERS
LEVEL Pre-1 BEGINNER
Rats
ANIMALS IN THE CITY
Ava Podmorow

ENGAGING READERS
LEVEL Pre-1 BEGINNER
Skunks
ANIMALS IN THE CITY
Ava Podmorow

Visit www.engagebooks.com/readers

Explore level 1 readers with the Animals That Make a Difference series.

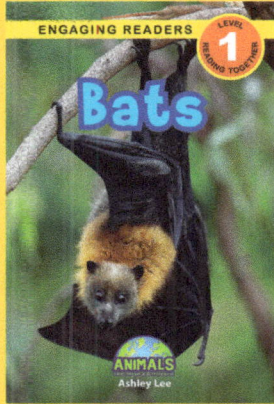

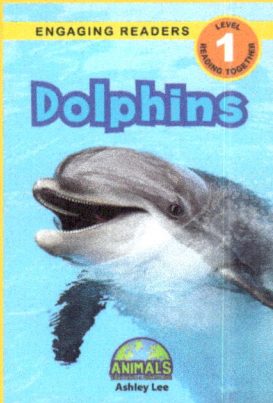

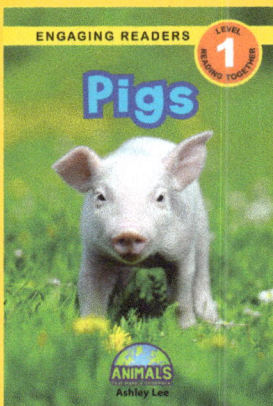

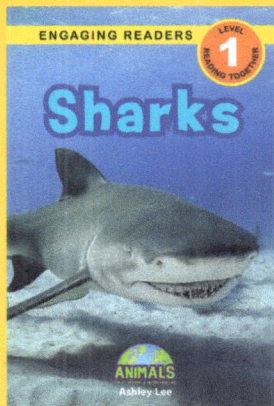

Bees
ENGAGING READERS — LEVEL 1 — READING TOGETHER
ANIMALS
Jared Siemens

Bats
ENGAGING READERS — LEVEL 1 — READING TOGETHER
ANIMALS
Ashley Lee

Birds
ENGAGING READERS — LEVEL 1 — READING TOGETHER
ANIMALS
Ashley Lee

Dolphins
ENGAGING READERS — LEVEL 1 — READING TOGETHER
ANIMALS
Ashley Lee

Horses
ENGAGING READERS — LEVEL 1 — READING TOGETHER
ANIMALS
Ashley Lee

Ladybugs
ENGAGING READERS — LEVEL 1 — READING TOGETHER
ANIMALS
Ashley Lee

Pigs
ENGAGING READERS — LEVEL 1 — READING TOGETHER
ANIMALS
Ashley Lee

Sharks
ENGAGING READERS — LEVEL 1 — READING TOGETHER
ANIMALS
Ashley Lee

Squirrels
ENGAGING READERS — LEVEL 1 — READING TOGETHER
ANIMALS
Ashley Lee

www.ingramcontent.com/pod-product-compliance
Lightning Source LLC
Chambersburg PA
CBHW051240020426
42331CB00016B/3457